PSEUDO-CHRISTIANS

PSEUDO-CHRISTIANS

RAY C. JARMAN

CHARISMA BOOKS
WATCHUNG, NEW JERSEY

©Copyright 1972

ISBN 0-912106-48-4

CHARISMA BOOKS
Watchung, N.J. 07060

Foreword

This book is not intended to be a comprehensive survey of the abstracted, intellectualized, and grossly compromised Christianity called Modernism, or the cults. For a scholarly work in this field I would recommend that you read Walter Martin's book, *The Kingdom of the Cults,* or the more popularly written, *The Chaos of the Cults* by J. K. Van Baalen, each of which is a detailed study of the major cults in America and some of the Modernism. And for a clear warning that the evil in them is real, read Hobart Freeman's *Angels of Light* (Logos) and Raphael Gasson's *The Challenging Counterfeit* (Logos).

My purpose is merely to point out the strong line that divides Modernism and the cults from the true Christianity that is taught in the Word of God. I will make no effort to annotate the statements, but only in a very simple and direct way to show where the cults and Modernism depart from the Word of God and what they lose of the promise of salvation that is so clearly contained in God's revelation.

I was myself for many years a Modernist. Feeling deeply the ineffectiveness of this philosophy and its utter failure to meet the needs of the people, and seeing how empty and purposeless and meaningless it was, I decided I had to find something else, a better answer.

So I departed from my colleagues and began to search in the cults, thinking that here I might find some reality. I saw that I was preaching the things that were indeed timely, but hardly timeless, contemporary, but not eternal. There was no reality, no living power in my message. Indeed, I was trying to help people to find some way to form a help-gaining relationship with whatever intelligence there is in back of the universe, and this intelligence I was trying to call God, but there was nothing clear in it. There was no clear way, no absolute assurance, no tangible gain. I had to have something. I began to search. I sought for my answer in the cults.

My studies in the universities had convinced me that the Bible was full of myths, legend, folklore, and contained many contradictions and superstitions that were brought up out of the minds of the people in their overzealous and superstitious minds. Therefore, I did not go to the Bible. It was nearly too late when I finally discovered that it is the only place that has the answer, but I began to search in the cults, in all the bewildering, seducing, blind alleys of Hell.

For eighteen years I taught Metaphysics (New Thought) over the radio every day, and sometimes as many as three times a day, and also in my very prosperous church. I was ordained to the ministry in 1913, and preached for fifty-two years until 1966, when I was past seventy, and then in a very miraculous moment I was born again in Christ and received that for which I had spent a lifetime-long searching.

Thank God the doubts are over! I know He is real. I am now able to see with spiritual eyes. Before, I could see only with the eyes of the intellect. I could see with the carnal mind, I could see with the natural mind, but I could not see with spiritual eyes, nor with the mind of the Spirit. Now I know that spiritual things are spiritually discerned, and thus in all my reading I was completely incapable of seeing real salvation, because my eyes were not opened to it.

Now it is not my purpose to condemn the Modernists and the cults. I merely want to point out what they are missing and what the great triumphant God is, when a man in his own heart comes to know Jesus Christ as his personal Savior.

We know that synthetic foods do not adequately nourish the body and very often deplete it; there are many people who are eating enough of the food, but there is no nourishment in it. The same thing is true in the realm of religion. There are synthetic religions trying to draw together all the religions of the world, but they do not have the power of God. They worship with their lips while their heart is far from Him; therefore, they bring about a people who are spiritually weak. Or they worship with the power of their own mind, committing the sin for which Lucifer himself was thrown out of Heaven.

I want to show you with this book, the strength that comes by feeding on the Word of God and knowing the Lord Jesus Christ as a personal living Savior, not an idea nor a great historic teacher, nor a state of mind, but as a person.

I want to show you that one of the great false assumptions in the field of religion and in reading the Bible, is that by intelligence everything in Heaven and on earth can be explained. This is not true; the Bible is a miracle of itself, and it cannot be explained by philosophy or psychology or anything else. It can only be explained by the fact that it is beyond intellectual comprehension; it is in the realm of the miraculous.

It is further my purpose to show that, had the church remained true to the Word of God, and placed its emphasis upon salvation, upon healing, and upon the Holy Spirit, such cults as Christian Science, Christian Unity, Christ Unity Science, Religious Science, Science of Divine Mind, Yoga, Theosophy, New Thought, would never have sprung into existence. For the real thing, I found, offers so *much more* than any counterfeit, that no one would choose the reflected light of the moon, when he could have the sun. And that very sun is but a pale reflection of the living Son of God.

I know. I found Jesus the hard way. Instead of looking for Him in the most obvious place of all, in the Word of God that I was preaching from, I sought not Him but 'meaning' and 'purpose' and 'spiritual experience' in the labyrinths of Hell. And there would I still be groping, alone and confused, had He not, in His infinite mercy, reached out and saved me.

SEARCHING

1

Searching

Driving down the street of any city or town, you will pass by many impressive church buildings, and out in the front you will see strong, heavy letters stating the denomination. All these buildings represent literally billions of dollars of the faithful and generous giving of Christian people. The stained-glass windows often depict events in the life of our Lord, or the overshadowing presence that is said to be with them. The pastor's name on the billboard in front of the church is often followed by the various academic degrees he has either been granted or has earned, to show that he is highly thought of and educated in the recognized theological seminaries of the land.

Now, if you are seeking help, and want to know how Jesus Christ can change your situation, can fill your life with meaning, you might think that this expensive church is the place to go, and this highly trained minister, the man to give you the answer you need. Indeed, if you want to know Jesus Christ, His death on the cross and the way His blood cleanses you from all sin and guilt, you might think that this learned pastor would not only have the answer, but would enthusiastically have it.

But this is often not the case. If you went to one of these churches with a facade that shouted its wealth and high denominational standing, the efficient secretary would probably direct you down the hall to a trained psychiatrist or counselor to first have certain psychological tests and a learned counselor tell you how to deal with your own life. After these tests you would be advised, for a fee, to come for more counseling. The fee may not be mentioned but the whole atmosphere will suggest it; so a thoughtful person will remember to do it and know that it is expected. The church, you will find, has its youth worker, home visitors, recreational facilities and directors. It is a place of endless activities and fellowship groups — programs for the elderly, for young couples, for singles, for teenagers and children. You will be fortunate indeed to ever gain an audience with the pastor himself.

But what about what you came for in the first place? What about Jesus and His saving power? Ask any member of the staff about this, and you'll get some cloudy answers, vague soothing statements worked out a long time ago, to the effect that modern education really has a more effective and intelligent answer than is ordinarily given by those who believe the Bible.

Now this is not the practice of every church, for God does have a remnant. God has always dealt with remnants, and these remnants oftentimes know the answer and give it unequivocally, but today they are but remnants.

The modern, highly trained, denominational preacher is most often a friendly, earnest person, trying to make his life effective and trying to make it effective with people, but if you could probe his heart you might see down there a deep dissatisfaction and frustration. He is trying so hard and feels he is not getting anyplace. There were over three thousand Protestant ministers who gave up the clergy last year and all of them gave substantially the same answer for their reason; they had become nothing more than "MC's in a religious club." They could not give their best because they did not know the best. Their main purpose was gathering new supporters, keeping the church in the black, and keeping themselves in the approval of the denominational authorities.

But, what about Jesus? Was He born like the Bible says He was? Did He die on the cross for you and me? Did He shed His blood so that we could be washed free of our sins, blameless before God?

To many workers these questions cannot be answered directly. They will begin to hedge, to suggest other meanings to the words, and to say that new discoveries about the Bible have revealed that these things in the Bible really are not to be taken literally, that we know that many of them are myths and legends that the early church built up. Oh yes, there was a Jesus. He was a good man. He was the greatest mind that ever lived and anyone who follows His ethical teachings will live the best possible life here and be saved for whatever life there may be after death.

Isn't it strange that the strongest and most devastating blows that are struck against Jesus and the Gospel, and the Word of God, are often struck in the very places where you would expect His highest acclaim? It's true now, and it was just as true in the day when Jesus came. The Pharisees and the Elders of the church were learned men. They knew the Scriptures. They knew how He was promised. They knew where He would be born. They knew that He would be the Son of God. But when He came, they didn't want to know Him; they struck against Him, and they crucified Him. So today, the learned pastors with advanced knowledge, finished training, polished messages, have no power of discernment. They have no Holy Spirit, and they do not believe in divine inspiration of the Word of God. They have so little to offer, and many thousands know it and are leaving, or staying away, from church.

The church finally becomes withered and plodding. They go through the ceremonies, follow an accurate calendar, christen the babies, marry the youths, visit the sick, give perfunctory prayers in the hospitals and bury the dead. And while the minister becomes more and more disillusioned and involved with church administration, the people are gradually dying on the vine, bringing forth no fruits of the Spirit. None of the gifts of the Spirit are in evidence. There is no enthusiastic participation, no healing of body, mind or spirit, no supernatural evidences. The church is lifeless. God *is* dead for the preacher, and often for the man in the pew. The hunger for the living God is dissuaded by the tradition that He is in the church, but really there is no evidence that He is there. You go away without feeling anything, seeing anything, or having anything happen to you. The disturbed minds and nervous people are sometimes calmed. The message of the pulpit is often how to endure sweetly and suffer the vicissitudes of life patiently, but there is no living Christ right there by your side, who will take you by the hand and lead you, no Holy Spirit to comfort you. The great and marvelous keeping care of God is overlooked. Again, this is not true of all churches, but it is true of many of them.

I write these things from sad experience, for I preached as a liberal Modernist for over fifty-two years. I traveled with them. I was educated by them. I was educated with them. I held the same views as thousands of modern ministers — men who hold many of the most outstanding influential churches in the land.

The Modernist preacher cannot accept the Biblical account of the Virgin Birth of Christ. He considers it one of the myths of the ages of the past, a myth that has come up out of other religions and is completely, scientifically impossible. And I quite agree with them; it *is* scientifically impossible. But name one thing that is impossible to God!

There is a red thread running through the Book of Genesis to the last page of Revelation, and it is made out of blood. In the Old Testament, it is the blood of the sacred lamb, without blemish and sacrificed by each family once a year, that the sins of the family may be forgiven for a year. That blood of the lamb is taken to the mercy seat and sprinkled upon it, absolving the family of sin and guilt for another year. It has meaning only because the Lamb is the Son of God, and He did it for all the people, everyone who would believe, because He said He loved us and all who would believe would not perish but have eternal life. He did it with His Only Begotten Son.

Many reject this whole story, and in doing so they take the very heart out of the Bible. They are religious people. They are good people. But they are not Christians. I would have considered it an affront, had anyone inferred that I was not a Christian, but after I found the Lord I realized that all the time I was not a Christian, for I did not believe these basic things in the Christian Scriptures.

Any other view becomes a creeping paralysis — when you reject the Virgin Birth, soon you reject other supernatural stories of the Bible and before long you have completely removed the power of God from your Bible. Then you are in company with men like Bultmann who sets in motion what he calls the "demythologizing the Bible." This leads us to the more serious problem of what part you are going to reject and what you are going to accept. Who shall be the judge of what is true and what isn't? What are the Modernist views? They contend that there is not a single passage in the Bible that you can put your finger on and say, "This is true." There is not a word in the Bible attributed to Jesus of which you can say, "Jesus said this." According to the higher critics you have nothing that Jesus said or did, but only what overzealous disciples reportedly said He said or did. What an unsteady foundation on which to build a faith! With this kind of teaching about the Bible, the whole Book dwindles into a few ethical, sociological teachings that were taught by Jesus.

I once held this position. My Bible was a book filled with myth, legend and folklore. I was convinced that the Bible was the record of the tribal God of a primitive people. I believed that the Bible had many inconsistencies and contradictions in it, and let me readily admit that intellectually it has. The biggest thing I learned when I was born again and was faced with the task of reevaluating my Bible, was that "spiritual things are spiritually discerned." Intellectually, the Bible is oftentimes confusing and baffling. I considered it the dullest book in the world. Now that I know the Lord, someone must have rewritten my Bible, because even the "begots" are interesting.

The Bible does not stand the test of science, psychology or

philosophy. Why? Because it is far above the knowledge of this world. You could have all the knowledge in the Library of Congress and still miss Jesus. The Bible is a miracle. To understand it, you must read it as a miracle. To read it as a miracle, you must be a miracle yourself, and when you are born again in Christ, you are a miracle. Before I could begin to grow as a new Christian, I had to see all the false things I had been teaching, and why I was in this error. I had been urging upon people things that were wrong and in error, and now I was upon the place that I must expose these errors. It was not easy to do. My new side caused me to see the errors I had made. I was appalled at the plain apostasy and actual agnosticism I had been teaching.

The reason so many earnest people have been leaving the orthodox church and looking elsewhere for spiritual meaning and reality, is that they have seen the spiritual apathy and confusion of Modernism. They have seen how both the preacher and the people have lost something. They are getting nothing, and they know it. Human beings simply cannot survive an empty and meaningless universe. Man is in rebellion against the lip-service ceremonies and sterile programs that the minister so often brings to them and calls it Christian religion. Never have I known more surely that this is really true. I realize that now I have a hard message to tell, but this message will bring reality and the power of God back into the lives of people. The harder it is, the more I praise God and thank Him for giving me the assignment of sharing it with you.

MY SEARCH FOR REALITY

2

My Search For Reality

When you know that there has got to be something more to life than the Modernist has to offer, else the gift of life itself is a travesty, you are going to search for that something more. Surely this can't be all, and when I was a Modernist teacher this idea just pressed against my mind constantly.

Arnold Toynbee, the great English historian, writes in his study of twenty-one civilizations, that nineteen of them vanished from the face of the earth, not by external forces, or from other nations conquering them, but because their people lost their faith in God, in their country, and themselves. And Spengler, another great historian, after the study of eleven civilizations that broke down and vanished, came to almost the identical conclusion.

What are we going to do as we see our own culture breaking down and falling to pieces? Can it really be laid at the door of the Modernist preacher who has taught something that doesn't have an adequate answer and filled the people with such emptiness and lack of meaning that they stagger before what is happening in the world and help to tear it apart?

One of our greatest errors is that we equate goodness, success and prosperity with salvation. Just because a man is good or because he is successful, or because he is a millionaire, we say, that man is pretty good, that man must have it, he's approved of God. Now just because a person is wearing a beautiful swimming suit does not mean that he is a good swimmer. And just because a person is informed on the Bible or carries the Bible, or tries to teach the Bible, and practices its ethical laws, does not mean that he is a Christian. Just because a man and his family attend church, take part regularly in its activities — he a member of the official board and she working with the women's guild, employed in every activity there is, prominent in all the church's work — does not mean that he or she is a Christian.

Read the story in the Bible. Two men went into the Temple to pray. Note that they both went to *pray,* so they were both practicing some of the things in the church. One of them was a Pharisee, the other a Publican. The Pharisee was a good man. The community believed he was good. The elders of the church rated him among the best, and he himself knew that he was good. He came down to the front of that church like a drum major. He was good, and in his prayers he reminded the Lord of just how good he was. He prayed thus with himself (I like that). He said, "Lord, I thank Thee that I am not as the rest of them; extortioners, unjust; adulterers or even as this Publican. I fast twice a week. I give tithes of all that I possess." He was a good man by any standards.

But the Publican who had done all the things the Pharisee boasted he had not done, struck the note of salvation. He said, "God be merciful to me, a sinner," and Jesus said that this man went down to his house justified rather than the other. To be justified means to be saved, covered with the righteousness of Jesus; therefore, this Publican was free from sin. He had exchanged his sin for the covering righteousness that Jesus provided. Jesus handed the new gown over to him as a cloak that covered him with salvation.

This is the teaching of the Bible. If you do not accept this teaching, your argument is not with me, but with the Bible. A church that teaches the Bible does not need to fear the cults. The abortive, freak religions come up to carry away the people who have not been taught the Gospel. Many fundamentalist churches are no better, for they follow the letter rather than the Spirit of the law and fail to have the compassion, mercy, grace and tenderness of God. They leave out the Grace of God and therefore the people still do not have anything that they can hold on to.

I was searching. My Bible had been hopelessly watered down by the Modernist professors. I could not find help there. I didn't believe in the divine inspiration of the Bible. I did not believe many stories in the Bible. Yet neither could I stand idly by while the hearts of the people were hungry for something more, something to satisfy the deep need of their souls. No matter what it cost me, I would search for a better message, though I knew my denominational colleagues would frown upon it. I would search in places where they wouldn't dare to be seen.

I went to see Dr. Holmes, the father of Religious Science. He introduced me to Troward and Quimby, Mary Baker Eddy, Goldsmith and also his own book, and I thought, Oh boy, now I've got it! All you have to do is to think right. The power of mind over matter. I learned about what they called Dynamic Power of a Single Thought; that you could move the universe by thinking strongly enough. You could turn an enemy around. You could move your life into success. You could destroy the particles of error in your body. You could get great wealth. You could achieve the proper partner. You could attain peace and happiness, all by the power of affirming and holding to a concentrated thought. You could be your own salvation. You could be like God.

Do you see that as long as Satan can keep your religion in your mind, no matter what you believe, he's got you? It has to move from the mind to the heart before you can defeat Satan. Out of the heart man believeth unto righteousness.

There is a fundamental error that is the basic foundation upon which all the Mental Science cults are built, and this error is also in Modernism. It is the fatherhood of God and the brotherhood of man. The omnipresence of God, that God is in everything. The cults build their hopes largely on the idea that there is a little bit of God in every person. The way to achieve God's power is through the power of concentration; to take hold of the indwelling God that is within you, and only by strong, firm, determination and thought, can you reach deeply enough into yourself to get hold of this power. If you do, you'll do something supernatural. You'll do something exceptional. You'll become a powerful person. Actually, it is just a sugar-coated humanism. The humanist philosopher would deny it, but this is what they teach: to lift yourself by your own bootstraps by getting hold of the God that is with you.

I once wrote a book on the great religions of the world, and there is one vast difference that distinguishes all other religions from Christianity. In all the oriental religions, it is self-realization. In Christian religion it is self-denial.

There is not a verse in the Bible that supports the idea that God is in everybody. God is not in anybody until they are born into His family. You have no right even to use the name of God until you are born into His family, just as you would not have a right to use my name unless you were born into my family, so you do not have a right to call God your Father until He really is your Father, by your having been born into His family, and you are then a member of His family and your name is written on the Lamb's Book of Life.

The Christian Unity and Mental Science group says, and sings a song, "I see the Christ in You." They go around trying to see the Christ in everybody no matter how evil the person is; they close their eyes a bit and look at the man and try to see the Christ in him, thinking that by seeing the Christ in him you'll bring it forth, and you will change your own attitude toward this violent offender. Well, if Christ is already in all of us why is He standing at the door and knocking? Why does He want to walk in where He has already entered? Jesus said, *"If* you abide in me, I will abide in you." He also said, *"If* a man love me, he will keep my word, and my Father will love him and we will come and make our abode in him."

I said to one teacher of Metaphysics, "Do you see the Christ in Hitler?" He had to say "yes." The whole foundation of his teaching would be destroyed if he didn't say yes, because they believe in this higher self that is in everybody. I continued to press him. "Do you see the Christ in Stalin?"

Stalin, by his own confession, admitted that he had murdered over ten million people. Yet the teacher said he saw the Christ in him. Then I said, "Do you see the Christ in that sex offender? The one who took that eight-year-old child out and molested her and then killed her?" And he said, "yes." How, then, could Jesus say to those Pharisees, as recorded in John 8:44, "Your Father is the devil"? Could God the Father abide in the same place?

The truth is that Christ is not in you until you are born in Him. John 1:12-13 says that as many as received Him, to them gave He the power to *become* the Sons of God, even to them that believe on His name, which were born not of blood nor the will of the flesh, nor the will of man, but of God. Jesus did not say that it would be a nice thing to have happen to you; you would be closer to God; you should try it. He said, "You *must* be born again." It is absolutely necessary.

All Modernists and all Modernist preachers, and all the Mental Science people, miss this plain command. They do not surrender themselves to the Lord Jesus Christ, accept His blood to wash away their sins and to restore their eternal life, and therefore they are outside of the family of God, and God has not come into them. They have not received the right to become children of God.

Millions of people are going to church today, and they think they are all right with God. They think that because they are good and are working in church, tithing, giving of their substance, teaching a Sunday school class, studying the Bible, that they're all right. Oh, my dear friends, this is not true. The Bible says, "Many will come to me in that day saying, Lord, Lord, did we not prophesy by thy name? Did we not cast out demons by thy name? And by thy name do many wonderful works?" Almost everybody would say that a person who had done things like that was certainly Christian, but Jesus said, "I will say to them, depart from me, ye that work iniquity. I never knew you" (Matt. 7:21-23).

I tried faithfully all the instructions in each of the Mental Science groups. I tried affirmations. I tried to follow the law and the principles. I didn't make very clear demonstrations, for they teach that everything in this universe operates according to law and principle. Jesus did no miracles. He merely knew the laws and principles of the universe better than we. If we knew the laws and principles as well as He, we could do everything He did and even greater things than He did. Our job then, is to learn what these laws and principles are and meditate upon them so that we can do these greater things.

It is a teaching of many of the Mental Science groups, and this includes Christian Science, sensitivity training, mind expansion, mind control, hypnotherapy, and so on, that Christ is a state of consciousness. Jesus became the Christ when He entered the highest consciousness, and He better and more completely than any other, so that when Peter looked at Him he said, "Thou art the Christ." But the Bible does not say that. The Bible says, "There is born to you this day in the City of David, a Savior who is Christ the Lord." He didn't become the Christ by entering into the highest consciousness. He was born Christ from the moment He took His first breath.

Another teaching within the Mental Science groups is a complete denial of the very core of the Bible, the very heart of the Word of God: there is no such thing as sin. Sin is only a mistake of mortal mind. They insist that God is Love. He is such love that He couldn't hurt you. He cannot even see sin, they say, for if He could, He couldn't be love. (Now, I don't know where they made that deduction, but that is the teaching.) If there is no such thing as sin, then there is no such thing as a Savior to die for our sins. Don't you see how clever the devil is? How cunning? He comes as an angel of light. He's beautiful. The Cross is the place where he suffered defeat, and if he can keep people from seeing that Cross and having been covered with that blood, he has accomplished a mighty victory. There's only one problem with that kind of teaching: it does not agree with the living Word of God. God not only sees sin, He punishes sin. The Bible says, "Oh, the goodness and severity of God." The whole plan of salvation is built upon the fact that man is depraved. His self-granted righteousness is as a filthy rag. Man is a sinner; he is under the curse of sin, and the only way he can be redeemed is to be born again under the power of the Lord Jesus Christ, to be covered with the blood of Jesus from Calvary. Without blood there is no forgiveness of sin. This is the place He redeemed us, on the Cross. Intellectually I don't understand this spiritual law. Spiritually I accept that it is a Holy Mystery, and that God did not intend for us to comprehend all His works. I just simply say that it is in the Bible, and if it is in the Bible, who am I to say that I know more than the Bible or any writer of it? But I'll also say something else: it's true. I know, because I have seen it work.

One teacher of Metaphysics reasons that sin is just taking hold of the wrong end of the right thing. In other words, it is all right to sin if you don't get dirty. He illustrates with a pen. If you take hold of the inky end, you'll get all dirty, but if you take hold of the other end you can write and draw or paint. The important thing is to get hold of the end that does not besmirch you. He reasons, evil is just "live" spelled backward. Devil is just "lived" spelled backward. Well, Serutan is "natures" spelled backward, so what? What does that mean? But, people who listen to this kind of teaching go away feeling they received a revelation.

Isn't it strange that people who are too smart to believe the Bible, can believe this kind of thing? The marvelous thing is, we can accept the blood of Jesus Christ and be cleansed of our sins, and this is a continual washing. Those who read His living Word and walk with Him are continually, day by day, cleansed by the blood of Christ. The Lord does not want us to sin, but the Bible tells us that if we do sin and heartily repent, we have an advocate with the Father, even Jesus Christ the Lord. So the greatest possible lawyer for the defense is with us continually, and He makes a plea for us before God. Who would want more?

Nothing in all the cults or the Mental Science groups can

match this. None has such promises. None can avail. The greatest proof of the Word of God and its reality is what happens when you take it away. It sends us scurrying around into all kinds of teachings; little broken threads of something we try to tie together, and to make into something that will help us, while we miss the powerful lifeline. And if we ever find our way back to it, as I did, the miracle occurs anew, and we lose our guilt before God, and stand as a miracle of God, washed from our sins.

THE BORN-AGAIN CHRISTIAN
HAS EVERYTHING

3

The Born-Again Christian Has Everything

Someone says, this sounds too easy. Well, it is. The man who has been deep in sin can't believe that just coming to Christ and repenting, and accepting the blood of Jesus, makes him free from sin, but that's what it is. It comes from the love and the grace and the desire of the great Heavenly Father to bring us back to Him. It's not His will that any of us should perish; therefore, He has provided a way for us to be redeemed, saved, and have eternal life. "By grace are you saved through faith. That not of yourselves. It is a gift of God" (Eph. 2:8).

It is all so wonderful, and it comes out of the deep, immeasurable love of God. It is not what we earn, for we never could earn it; it is what God gives because He loves us. Paul tells us that "the weapons of our warfare are not carnal, but mighty through God to the pulling down of . . . imaginations, and every high thing that exalteth itself against the knowledge of God, and bringing into captivity every thought to the obedience of Christ" (II Cor. 10:4-5) KJV.

There is no one thing that is promised by the Mental Science groups that is not promised in far greater abundance to the born-again Christian.

Take sickness for example. The Mental Science groups have persuaded great multitudes that they have the only panacea for all sickness and all healing, and their answer is to just believe it doesn't exist. But if you hit your finger with a hammer, you know it hurts, no matter what you say. In Mental Science, people say all sickness is an error of mortal mind. Affirm your health; get a mental picture of your health; hold to it in spite of your feeling. Bodily suffering has no need for a physician. It will disappear if you think right. They contend that there is no power known to man greater than a thought strong in health.

Satan can counterfeit the gifts of the Spirit, even healing. The Mental Science groups do achieve certain results, and they publish them abroad, but there are millions of followers that demonstrate nothing. They go away empty-handed. One person said to me that Christian Science has been approved of God. Jesus said, (and I say this again to you) in Matthew 7:22-23, "Many will come to me saying, Lord, Lord, have we not prophesied by Thy Name; by Thy Name cast out demons; by Thy Name done mighty works? Then will I say unto them, I never knew you. Depart from me ye workers of iniquity."

So you can do many wonderful things in the name of Jesus, and still be a worker of iniquity, completely unknown to Him. Such works are not anything to prove that you are a Christian. If you are known to God, you must be born into His family, accepted of Jesus; you must realize that He came in the flesh as God manifest among you, who died for your sins and that the Father raised Him from the dead. Then you are known to Him and rewarded by Him. These are the very things that the Mental Science people reject or abstract, and make them mean something entirely different from what the Bible says.

If you want to see real miracles of physical healing of people completely given up by doctors, go to Bible-believing Christians. In their churches I have seen things happen that I believed could not happen, and when they did happen, I was filled with incredulity and amazement. Not everyone is healed. I don't know why. If I did, I would be as God. Want case histories? Read Kathryn Kuhlman's book, *God Can Do It Again.*

The power of God to heal the body is the same as the power of God to heal in sin. The only difference is that if you come to God for forgiveness of sins, you *always* get it. Everyone is freed from his guilt, and Mental Science cannot touch that. Jesus taught that God has the power to do both—heal the body and heal the heart from guilt and sin. Once He cried to Simon the Pharisee, "Which is easier to say, thy sins be forgiven thee, or to say arise and take up thy bed and walk? But that you may know that the Son of God has power on earth to forgive sins—" Then He said to the sick of the palsy, "Arise and take up thy bed and go into thy house, and the sick of the palsy arose and took up his bed and walked" (Matt. 9:5-7).

No one in the church has the power to heal anyone, but Jesus has, and members of the church are His servants. Therefore, they see people rise, take up their bed and walk, and they see thousands of people born again in Christ and freed from their sins. Everyone who comes to Him and asks, receives this miracle. Therefore, they can say, rise and walk. They can say, "My sins are forgiven—Praise the Lord."

The Mental Science people, New Thought, treat the Bible like a cafeteria. They hurry through the Bible, tray in hand, and select the things that seem good to them or can be bent around to support their teachings, and leave the rest. If you ever hear one of them quote from Scripture, check your Bible and see what it actually says, and what it really means in context.

For example, the Mental Science teachers ring all the changes on the statement: "You shall know the truth, and the truth shall make you free." They contend that truth is knowledge, and wherever you learn the truth it sets you free from so much ignorance. But go to your Bible and read what it says. John 8:1-32 reads: "Then said Jesus to those Jews *who believed in Him,* if you *continue* in my Word, then are you truly my disciples, and you shall know the truth and the truth shall make you free." Read the whole sentence. What is the Word? The Word became flesh and dwelt among us. What is the truth? Jesus is the truth. It is not knowledge that sets you free, but Jesus. And verse 36 clinches it: "And if the Son shall set you free, you shall be free indeed." How could anything be plainer?

Well, we could write a whole book on the way plain and

understandable verses of the Bible are lifted out of context and distorted by the "New-Thoughters." The Bible is either true or it is not true. We do not have to interpret it. We just have to read it. When we learn to read the Bible for just what it says and not what someone tells us it says, then the Bible will become increasingly clear to us. Wouldn't it be a strange God who would write us a living revelation to judge us by, and then make it too difficult for us to read and understand? The Bible is a simple book, and it means exactly what it says. Not anything less, nor anything more, but just exactly what it says. "A wayfaring man, though a fool, need not err therein" (Isa. 35:8). To go through the Bible and say that each time it says Father or Son, it means conscious and subconscious mind; and where it says Father, Son, and Holy Ghost, it means conscious, subconscious and superconscious mind, is a calculated attack against God and His Word, and God will hold a person who does that responsible. And then, when it says five . . . five husbands or five fish, five loaves . . . that it means the five senses, is also a travesty upon God and one will certainly be held accountable for it. Doesn't it make sense that God knows enough to say in plain, understandable words, what He wants to say to His children?

Let me give you another example. In the Christian Unity organization, they take some of the most sacred Scriptures and make parodies of them that are offensive to anyone who looks upon the Bible as the inspired Word of God. They take the beloved Twenty-Third Psalm, for example, and turn it into a psalm of crass materialism, of utter selfishness and self-centeredness, and the way for one to obtain wealth. Now while God is going to take care of His children, there is certainly a curse upon anybody who would change His revealed words to say something else. And all those people carrying such a word as this around in their pockets, are carrying a curse upon their lives, because the Word of God sends a curse upon anybody who will change or alter the revealed word. Take this for example:

"The Lord is my Banker; my credit is good. He maketh me

to lie down in the consciousness of the omnipotent abundance; He giveth me the key to His strong box. He restoreth my faith in His riches; He guides me in the paths of prosperity for His name's sake. Yea though I walk through the very shadow of death, I shall fear no evil, for Thou art with me; Thy silver and gold, they secure me. Thou preparest a way for me to be in the presence of the collector; Thou fillest my wallet with money; my treasure runneth over. Surely goodness and plenty will follow me all the days of my life; and I shall do business in the name of the Lord forever" (Published in *Christian Unity*).

There's something sick in the mind of anybody who can take some of the most beautiful passages that we know, and turn them into one of the most selfish, self-centered, and greed-filled ideas, in order to make a people believe that they can fill their pockets by saying these words. This is an example of turning the Word of God and making it say what was never intended. But all one has to do is to read the Sunday-school literature that is printed by this organization and see how the Bible is distorted and changed, rewritten in many places, to realize how far away one can get from the revealed Word of God. I found that these people were promising what they could not and did not deliver. So I began seeking in other places.

SEARCHING IN THE OCCULT

4

Searching In The Occult

I tried Yoga. You know, as I look through the teaching of Yoga, the thing that amazes my mind is, how is it possible that a person who contends he is too intelligent to believe the Bible, can believe things like this? Statement after statement, with nothing more than just a statement; nothing to prove it; no evidence shown; just a rehearsing in our occidental life of oriental mysticism until some people wither and die in their soul. "Fear not him who destroys the body, but who can destroy the body and the soul."

These people dress in robes and sit around and try to attain what they call Samati, which is universal oneness: oneness with the flowers, oneness with the birds, oneness with the clouds, oneness with the airplanes, oneness with the telephone poles. I don't know what the purpose of it is other than just by concentrated thinking to escape from the demands of reality. But Jesus *is* reality.

These people believe that there are many masters. They are nice enough to say that Jesus was one of the masters. I have news for these people. Jesus wasn't *one* of the masters. He was *the* Master.

After Yoga, I moved to Theosophy. I learned all about cosmic consciousness, and I learned about reincarnation. Theosophy numbers the world in terms of millions and millions of years and various stages of races and developments of races, periods of time. Theosophists even spend much time in the study of the great Atlantic Ocean which was supposed to have contained the continent of Atlantis. They also study Lemuria in the Pacific Ocean. And these lost civilizations were far beyond the civilization we have today, but under a global convulsion were completely destroyed. They tried to search to find out what the philosophies and teachings and the ancient manuscripts about this immense antiquity contained for us. They laid great emphasis on the teaching that God is in everybody. There's a fragment of God, of divinity, in every person, and if the initiate gets hold of this divinity, he can bring forth great ideas and great things superior to others. They count in millions the reincarnations that have come and gone into the development of this particular hour and they hold that we are the reincarnation of somebody in a past life or lives.

Of course this is nothing but oriental mysticism. There is no proof of it. It is beautiful. I don't know of any philosophy that is more attractive than reincarnation. For example, the inequities of life. Why is it that one person is born with a silver spoon in his mouth and another is born in poverty? Why is it that one person is born with a high I.Q., and another has a low I.Q.? Why is it that one person is born and before he is two or three years of age he is almost a finished musician and from then on produces the finest of music, while someone else may study music all his life and never be able to write a single note of it, or do much about it? Reincarnation has an answer to many of these things. Reincarnation has an answer to the reason someone is born with a terribly distorted body, and another person is born with a perfectly beautiful, marvelous body. Their explanation is that the distorted body is a reincarnation of someone who existed earlier and did a very sinful thing in distorting the body of somebody else in a former life, and he's paying the debt for it now.

You see, if you believe in reincarnation, you must believe in the law of karma, which is the law of cause and effect; that when you are born, you are born with your karmic debt upon you. This is the place where the devil, through this clever and cunning device, moves people away from the central truth, the Word of God, teaching that man is a sinner

- 38 -

and that Jesus Christ died on the Cross, that his sins may be forgiven.

According to the doctrine of reincarnation, man is a sinner. He has his karmic debt upon himself for the sins he has committed in former lives, and he is here to pay the debt for the sins he formerly committed. You see, in the oriental world, life was so terrible, so hard, so distressing and magic, that the explanation that was given to it was that all this suffering and all this hardship was to pay a debt for former lives, and the best thing that could possibly happen to anybody would be that he would come to the time that he would never have to live again. He wouldn't have to go through this suffering. He wouldn't have to go through all these trials and heartaches, and heartbreaking situations. He would be free from living.

So they said that as you live one life after another, you are paying the debt for the sins you have committed in former lives. When you die you go up to a court of review someplace where they show you who you are; how many lives you have lived; what your names were; what kind of sins you committed; and how much progress you have made in paying the debt for those sins in the last life you lived. Then you are sent back on the wheel of rebirth, not once, but hundreds of times, until finally you have paid in full for all your sins. Then you go into the sea of nirvana. Nirvana means oblivion. I don't know who wants it, but it appears to be the best gift the reincarnationists have to offer.

If you can pay the debt for your sins by your lives, what was the purpose of Jesus dying on the Cross for your sins? Satan was beaten at that Cross. He doesn't want anyone to believe in this, or even to go near it, so he comes through with one of the most clever, cunning things you have ever read about in your life. The devil appears as an angel of light, and he leads us according to the path he makes, and he makes it look so beautiful that we think we're going in the direction which will be for us the release from all things which cause us distress.

But Jesus came to release us from our sins, and to free us from the curse of Adam that is upon us, so that we could enter back into eternal life, which is the natural heritage of God's children. The reincarnationists teach all about astral planes, mental bodies, and how it is possible to leave this physical body and dwell in the astral world and meet and talk with those who have gone on before us. In this sense they are very close to spiritualism and all the other nonsense that goes along with the Psychic. Many very intelligent people seem to persuade themselves that they have received something of value, but it leads them away from God. Actually it is a satisfaction to the guilty heart to be led away from the convicting presence of Jesus.

Just as Theosophy is esoteric, the thing which is hidden, Spiritism is exoteric, the thing which is revealed. I delved around in Theosophy for a long time, visited many of its centers, listened to its lecturers, but from my own mind I could not receive any warmth, any love. I realized it was just an objective attempt to study out through the mind something to hold onto, to grasp at, to save one from the sordidness, strife and competition of the world in which we live.

So I tried Spiritism. I went to many Spiritualist meetings. I found that great numbers of the Spiritualist mediums were quacks and charlatans. I found a small percentage of them do have some demonic power, demonstrably from Satan. Read Raphael Gasson's *The Challenging Counterfeit* (Logos).

There are many texts in the Bible to show you that God condemns all kinds of Spiritism. At this point I will include some of the passages of Scripture (KJV) that strongly condemn all Spiritism, fortune-telling, false prophets, automatic writing, astrology and the whole field of the Psychic.

EXODUS
22:18   Thou shalt not suffer a *witch* to live.

LEVITICUS

19:26   Ye shall not eat any thing with the blood: neither shall ye use *enchantment* (hypnosis), nor *observe times* (astrology).

19:31   Regard not them that have *familiar spirits* (mediums), neither seek after wizards, to be defiled by them: I am the Lord your God.

20:6   And the soul that turneth after such as have *familiar spirits*, and after *wizards* (magicians), to go a whoring after them, I will even set my face against that soul, and will cut him off from among his people.

20:27   A man also or woman that hath a *familiar spirit*, or that is a *wizard*, shall surely be put to death: they shall stone them with stones: their blood shall be upon them.

DEUTERONOMY

17:2-5   If there be found among you, within any of the gates which the Lord thy God giveth thee, man or woman, that hath wrought wickedness in the sight of the Lord thy God, in transgressing his covenant, and hath gone and served other gods, and worshipped them, either the sun, or moon, or any of the *host of heaven* (constellations), which I have not commanded; And it be told thee, and thou hast heard of it, and enquired diligently, and, behold, it be true, and the thing certain, that such abomination is wrought in Israel: Then shalt thou bring forth that man or that woman, which have committed that wicked thing, unto thy gates, even that man or that woman, and shalt stone them with stones, till they die.

18:9-15 When thou art come into the land which the Lord thy God giveth thee, thou shalt not learn to do after the abominations of those nations. There shall not be found among you any one that maketh his son or his daughter to pass through the fire, or that useth *divination* (clairvoyant or seer), or an *observer of times* (astrology), or an *enchanter*, or a *witch*, or a *charmer*, or a *consulter with familiar spirits*, or a *wizard*, or a *necromancer* (medium who consults the dead). *For all that do these things are an abomination unto the Lord:* and because of these abominations the Lord thy God doth drive them out from before thee. Thou shalt be perfect with the Lord thy God. For these nations, which thou shalt possess, hearkened unto *observers of times,* and unto *diviners:* but as for thee, the Lord thy God hath not suffered thee so to do. The Lord thy God will raise up unto thee a Prophet from the midst of thee, of thy brethren, like unto me; unto him ye shall hearken; –

II KINGS

9:22   And it came to pass, when Joram saw Jehu, that he said, Is it peace, Jehu? And he answered, What peace, so long as the whoredoms of thy mother Jezebel and her *witchcrafts* are so many?

17:16-17   And they left all the commandments of the Lord their God, and made them molten images, even two calves, and made a grove, and worshipped all the host of heaven, and served Baal. And they caused their sons and their daughters to pass through the fire, and used *divination* (fortune-telling, Ouija boards, glass-tumbler moving, tea-leaf reading, palm reading, ESP, telepathy, numerology) and *enchantments,* and sold themselves to do evil in the sight of the Lord, to provoke him to anger.

21:2-6   And he (Manasseh) did that which was evil in the sight of the Lord, after the abominations of the heathen, whom the Lord cast out before the children of Israel. For he built up again the high places which Hezekiah his father had destroyed; and he reared up altars for Baal, and made a grove, and did as Ahab king of Israel; and worshipped all *the host of heaven,* and served them. And he built altars in the house of the Lord, of which the Lord said, In Jerusalem will I put my name. And he built altars for all *the host of heaven* in the two courts of the house of the Lord. And he made his son pass through the fire, and *observed times,* and used *enchantments,* and dealt with *familiar spirits* and wizards: he wrought much wickedness in the sight of the Lord, to provoke him to anger.

23:24   Moreover, the workers with *familiar spirits,* and the *wizards,* and the images, and the idols, and all the abominations that were spied in the land of Judah and in Jerusalem, did Josiah put away, that he might perform the words of the law which were written in the book that Hilkiah the priest found in the house of the Lord.

I CHRONICLES

10:13-14   So Saul died for his transgression which he committed against the Lord, even against the word of the Lord, which he kept not, and also for asking counsel of one that had a *familiar spirit,* to enquire of it; And enquired not of the Lord: therefore he slew him, and turned the kingdom unto David the son of Jesse.

ISAIAH

8:19   And when they shall say unto you, Seek unto them that have *familiar spirits,* and unto *wizards* that peep, and that mutter: should not a people seek unto their God? for the living to the dead?

47:9   But these two things shall come to thee in a moment in one day, the loss of children, and widowhood: they shall come upon thee in their perfection for the multitide of thy *sorceries,* and for the great abundance of thine *enchantments.*

47:12-14   Stand now with thine *enchantments,* and with the multitude of thy *sorceries,* wherein thou hast laboured from thy youth; if so be thou shalt be able to profit, if so be thou mayest prevail. Thou art wearied in the multitude of thy counsels. Let now the *astrologers,* the *stargazers,* the monthly *prognosticators,* stand up, and save thee from these things that shall come upon thee. Behold they shall be as stubble; the fire shall burn them; they shall not deliver themselves from the power of the flame: there shall not be a coal to warm at, nor fire to sit before it.

JEREMIAH

8:1-2   At that time, saith the Lord, they shall bring out the bones of the kings of Judah, and the bones of his princes, and the bones of the priests, and the bones of the prophets, and the bones of the inhabitants of Jerusalem out of their graves: And they shall spread them before the sun, and the moon, and all *the host of heaven,* whom they have loved, and whom they have served, and after whom they have walked, and whom they have sought, and whom they have worshipped: they shall not be gathered, nor be buried; they shall be for dung upon the face of the earth.

14:14   Then the Lord said unto me, The prophets prophesy lies in my name: I sent them not, neither have I commanded them, neither spake unto them: they prophesy unto you a false vision and *divination*, and a thing of nought, and the deceit of their heart.

19:13   And the houses of Jerusalem, and the houses of the kings of Judah, shall be defiled as the place of Tophet, because of all the houses upon whose roofs they have burned incense unto all *the host of heaven*, and have poured out drink offerings unto other gods.

27:9-10   Therefore hearken not ye to your prophets, nor to your *diviners*, nor to your *dreamers*, nor to your *enchanters*, nor to your *sorcerers*, which speak unto you, saying, Ye shall not serve the king of Babylon: For they prophesy a lie unto you, to remove you far from your land; and that I should drive you out, and ye should perish.

29:8-9   For thus saith the Lord of hosts, the God of Israel; Let not your prophets and your *diviners*, that be in the midst of you, deceive you, neither hearken *to your dreams* which ye cause to be *dreamed*. For they prophesy falsely unto you in my name: I have not sent them, saith the Lord.

ZEPHANIAH

1:4-6   I will also stretch out my hand upon Judah, and upon all the inhabitants of Jerusalem; and I will cut off the remnant of Baal from this place, and the name of the Chemarims with the priests; And them that worship *the host of heaven* upon the house tops; and them that worship and that swear by the Lord, and that swear by Malcham; And them that turned back from the Lord; and those that have not sought the Lord, nor enquired for him.

ACTS

16:16-18   And it came to pass, as we went to prayer, a certain damsel possessed with *a spirit of divination* met us, which brought her masters much gain by soothsaying: The same followed Paul and us, and cried saying, These men are the servants of the most high God, which shew unto us the way of salvation. And this did she many days. But Paul, being grieved, turned and said *to the spirit*, I command thee in the name of Jesus Christ to come out of her. And *he* came out the same hour.

19:19   Many of them also which used *curious arts* bought their books together, and burned them before all men: and they counted the price of them, and found it fifty thousand pieces of silver.

GALATIANS

3:1-3 O Foolish Galatians, who hath *bewitched* you, that ye should not obey the truth, before whose eyes Jesus Christ hath been evidently set forth, crucified among you? This only would I learn of you, Received ye the Spirit by the works of the law, or by the hearing of faith? Are ye so foolish? having begun in the Spirit, are ye now made perfect by the flesh?

4:10-11 *Ye observe days, and months, and times, and years.* I am afraid of you, lest I have bestowed upon you labour in vain.

5:19-21 Now the works of the flesh are manifest, which are these; Adultery, fornication, uncleanness, lasciviousness, Idolatry, *witchcraft,* hatred, variance, emulations, wrath, strife, seditions, heresies, Envyings, murders, drunkenness, revellings, *and such like;* of which I tell you before, as I have told you in time past, that *they which do such things shall not inherit the kingdom of God.*

REVELATION

9:20-21 And the rest of the men which were not killed by these plagues yet repented not of the works of their hands, that they should not worship devils, and idols of gold, and silver, and brass, and stone, and of wood; which neither can see, nor hear, nor walk: Neither repented they of their murders, *nor of their sorceries,* nor of their fornication, nor of their thefts.

18:23 And the light of a candle shall shine no more at all in thee; and the voice of the bridegroom and of the bride shall be heard no more at all in thee: for thy merchants were the great men of the earth; *for by thy sorceries* were all nations deceived.

21:8 But the fearful, and unbelieving, and the abominable, and murderers, and whoremongers, *and sorcerers,* and idolaters, and all liars shall have their part in the lake which burneth with fire and brimstone: *which is the second death.*

There are many more such Scriptures to be found in the Bible, the Word of God. Really, the strongest of all is the very first commandment of the Bible: "Thou shalt have no other gods before me." And when we even "in fun" turn to Spiritism, or to any of these cults, or to a hypnotist, or the Ouija board, divination, or astrology, or any of these things, we are actually telling God that He hasn't got quite enough for us, and God has all that you need. All you need is Jesus. Whenever you go to dealing with the Psychic, you are inviting discarnate spirits to live in your body.

I know people who say that a medium "told me things she had no way of knowing. How do you account for that?" Satan has access to our minds if we admit him by disobeying God, and I can tell you what will happen.

In Ft. Lauderdale, Florida, a woman called up and said, "Dr. Jarman, I'm a member of the Presbyterian church, and my husband died, and I was so filled with grief that I was practically morbid, and no one could comfort me. Finally someone persuaded me to go to a spiritualist medium. I went and came home walking on cloud nine because I was convinced I had been talking to my husband. He told me things that only he and I knew. This clinched it, so I began going regularly to spiritualists, but oh, Dr. Jarman, what has happened since! There are knockings on the walls. There are knockings on my bed in the night. Dishes jump off of the pantry shelf, break on the floor." Even while I was talking to her, I could hear a dish crash to the floor. Satan's demons are legion; they delight in bedeviling foolish psychic dabblers.

Do you want to live in a world like that? You see, Satan knows what causes sickness, because he induced it. So, he will tell a person like Edgar Cayce at first, what caused the sickness and how to heal it, thus gathering people away from Jesus, to believe in something else — anything to destroy your belief and confidence in the Word of God.

Edgar Cayce, for example, was a Sunday-school teacher, but he did not know the born-again experience. He became interested in hypnotism, somebody hypnotized him, and an evil spirit came into him. Thereafter, every time he lay down, this evil spirit began talking through him. Cayce himself was utterly surprised and astonished at what was being said, because it was somebody else, an evil spirit that had taken hold of him.

The devil gave Cayce enough information to convince thousands of people, who would send him their symptoms so that he could diagnose what was ailing them. Then he would send back the remedy they should take. He, or rather the spirit which possessed him, also advised people on financial investments. A few got rich, others lost all the money they had. He himself died practically in poverty, under indictment of the court.

Health and wealth — what more could anyone ask for, except possibly the two things that Satan could never counterfeit: Salvation and Eternal Life. Yet today Cayce is looked upon by gullible thousands as some kind of secular prophet.

A Prophet of God is always right. Remember that. A man who is not a Prophet of God is wrong many many times, because the devil is wrong. But God's Prophets are always right. The same thing is true of Jeane Dixon. She claims to be the Prophet of this day, yet she herself admits that she is 35 percent wrong, and those who have studied her, say she is closer to 65 percent wrong.

If she's a Prophet of God, she's right and always right. Never wrong at any place, because God cannot be wrong. If she is not a Prophet of God, then I leave it to you to decide whose prophet she is.

The same thing is true of the spiritualist mediums. King Saul went to the Witch of Endor against God's command, and he forfeited his life the next day for it. God does not want us to go to anybody else but Himself. He has given us the channel of prayer. He has given us the power to communicate with and be with, and be guided from the Lord Jesus Christ. That is all we need. That is the source of our greatest power.

Now, the same thing is true about the Ouija board. The Ouija board is outselling Monopoly as a 'harmless' game, yet it brings evil wherever it is. I wouldn't have one of them even stored away in my home, because an evil spirit is residing within that board. A scientist one time said to me, "You don't mean to tell me that an inanimate thing is animated?" I said to him, "You know that all things are made up of atoms and these atoms are moving in a certain rhythm that makes them appear like this, and between atoms there is space. That space can be occupied by an evil spirit."

We worry about the effect of television on the minds of children, but if you have a child in your home who is sensitive to a Ouija board, it may affect his life for the rest of his days. If you have a Ouija board, get it out and burn it up. Don't give it to anybody. Burn it up.

The same thing is true of astrology. You can't publish a newspaper these days unless it has a regular horoscope column in it. Many people are actually bound, being held by the predictions that are in astrological tables shown in our newspapers. They won't go out the door in the morning, make a purchase, go to their job, until they find out what their horoscope says. God is free. God gives freedom. He doesn't give limitations.

Look at Noah, building the Ark, as he tried to tell the people how they could be saved. They went to their astrologers. Their astrologers made all kinds of fun, but the day came when they went to the astrologers, and the astrologers had to say, "Don't ask us. We're going to have to save ourselves!"

Look at Jeremiah. He advised the people and told them what was going to happen. They wouldn't listen to him. They went to the astrologers and the high priests, and the astrologers and high priests told them what they wanted to hear; consequently their lives were destroyed. This is the constant, repeated story, yet man never seems to learn.

When we go to these things, I repeat yet again, we are going to something else as a substitute for going to God, preferring them to Him, in direct disobedience to the first, as well as the Great Commandment. Why is it so serious?

Because anything supernatural that is not of God is of Satan, that's why. It is just that simple, just that clear-cut a choice between black and white. So the next time you might be tempted to dabble in ESP or fortune-telling or hypnosis or Ouija or any of the so-called 'harmless' spook-and-kook pursuits, just remember that you are toying with the well-being of your immortal soul!

There's another thing that is very true in this area and often not observed. Following all forays into Mental Science, cults and the occult, are periods of deep depression. Sometimes a person may have left the forbidden areas for some time, may be trying to seek salvation and can't receive it, can't receive the Holy Spirit, can't be sure within himself that he really has been born again in Christ. And it is because one of these discarnate spirits has been permitted to enter and is living in the body and creating an atmosphere of depression and oppression. It grows deeper and deeper until the person just simply can't stand it. They can't understand. They say . . . I pray, I ask God to help me, and I get no answer.

Perhaps in his home he has a lot of metaphysical literature, and that material is a denial of the deity of Christ as recorded in the Word of God. They do not believe in sin. They do not believe that the blood of Jesus Christ had the efficacy to wash sin away. This is at the heart of the Bible, and therefore the people who have the teaching of the cults and the reading materials in their homes, are calling down the wrath of God upon themselves. To have on your bookshelves something that denies the Only Begotten Son, denies you the blessings of God and cannot be pleasing to God. So have a blessed book-burning. God wants us to make a complete and full surrender to Him, and that means we are to get away from all of these apostasies, even these roots that are offsprings from Christian religions themselves, but have left out the real, great, important thing in the Bible.

We must hold on with all of our spiritual strength to the center, the heart of the Bible. It is the heart of the Bible that the Modernist denies. It is the heart of the Bible that is denied in Christian Science, in Religious Science, Mental Science, Theosophy, Sensitivity Training, Yoga, all the rest of them. And what is that? That man is a sinner. That every man is under the curse of Adam's sin. He is utterly depraved. There is no good thing in him. His righteousness is as filthy rags. The heart of the Bible is that God provides a way for all this guilt and sin and depravity to be taken away and for man to be born again in Jesus Christ. And, how can he be born again in Jesus Christ? He can be born again only through receiving the blood of Jesus Christ as the Atonement shed for his sins, and accepting Jesus, repenting before Him for his own sins and asking for forgiveness, and accepting the blood of Jesus to wash him clean. This is the heart of the Bible.

If you try to analyze it intellectually, you will only be frustrated. Spiritual things are spiritually discerned, and the plane of spiritual understanding is above intelligence; it is above all knowledge, above all philosophy and psychology. It is in the realm of the miraculous. It's the miracle of God. That God so loved the world that He gave his Only Begotten Son, that whosoever *believeth in Him* should not perish but have everlasting life. It is not whosoever makes an affirmation; nor whosoever goes into a higher consciousness, nor whosoever finds what there may be said to be Heaven that is called God, who is saved. No, not that at all, but whosoever believeth in Jesus, believeth in the sense of adhering to Him, accepting Him, and holding onto Him. That person receives salvation.

Do you know what has kept us from seeing and dwelling in this major thing, this heart of the Bible? Well, when we get born again we are told we ought to read the Bible, and we begin to read it, and the first thing you know we find some particular thing that is interesting to us, and we go all through the Scriptures searching for that particular thing. Maybe it is the Kingdom of God. Maybe it's Manifest Sons of God. Maybe it's ultimate reconciliation. Maybe it's eternal security. Maybe it's the Armenian theory. Maybe it's worshiping on the seventh day. Maybe it's the form of baptism.

But, when we do this, our attention often gets sidetracked, and so does the main issue: determination to know God and to know Jesus Christ and Him crucified on the Cross. And when we get away from the heart of the Bible, immediately there's an oppression, a darkness that begins to settle upon us, and in the midst of this darkness, we are looking around.

Then almost anything that comes by will cause us to grasp onto it. And that's the reason that many, many people seeking God go off on some of these cults, because they're not getting satisfaction. The church is not helping them, not meeting their need. They are going out of the church empty and unfulfilled, because they have in their minds and their reading a lot of things that are extraneous to the central thing in the Bible.

Remember one thing; Jesus died on the Cross for you to free you from guilt, from the curse of Adam, from the filthiness of your own righteousness, and to lift you up as a Son of God.

There are a lot of other things in the Bible, and sometimes you'll be disturbed by some stories in the Old Testament that appear to be far from the moral standards that you yourself hold. You'll come to the time when you'll understand those things too, but because we are just babes in Christ, we bring our own worldly traditions and training to bear upon these stories, and we often come away dissatisfied and frustrated. Whereas, if you just look to the central thing, you can't exhaust it, you can't overdescribe it, you can't overdo it, this central thing: that God provided a way for you to be saved, that God provided a way to lift your guilt so that you should never feel guilty again. He washes you with the blood of Jesus Christ, the only detergent known to man that can wash away sins. He cleanses you. He makes you pure. He makes you whiter than snow. He makes you holy in the sight of God. And which one of us doesn't want that?

But in order to have it, we must free ourselves from all extraneous things. Many things seem to be good in themselves. There can't be anything wrong about this, we say, and we begin to follow, but we are going down a dead-end street and not staying on the main highway. Suddenly as we get way down the street, we find we are getting no place, and then a deep depression follows, and we move in an aura of overwhelming gloom.

You know, Satan is darkness. Whenever darkness begins to come, it is never of God, because in Him there is no darkness at all. So, whenever Satan begins to come, we feel in the dark, and we begin searching ourselves; a heavy load is upon us, and we can scarcely breathe. And our imagination — oh, the sins of vain imaginings! We imagine this, that, and the other. We exaggerate everything into some negative possibility, and of course the Mental Science people come along and try to lift us out of this by telling us to think positively, and to try all those little gimmicks, in order to lift us away from this thing that is holding onto us like glue. But it makes no difference what they say. These oppressions come, and they come to stay. There is only one way to lift an oppression and that is to receive Jesus Christ and to know He has the power to cleanse you from sin; and when you receive Him, then you have this miracle occur in you so that the oppression is gone forever.

In all fields of learning — it doesn't make any difference what area of thought you are surveying — people are looking for something that will modify everything that they already know, and consequently, nobody is quite certain. Nothing in the world is quite so uncertain as the field of psychology. Those who are studying in that area, come back with different ideas, different opinions, and all the time the whole structure of psychology is being changed, altered, modified. But when you have found Jesus Christ, He's the same yesterday, today and forever. You are not looking around for something different. You *know* you have the Truth. Your belief is unshakable.

"Whosoever heareth these words of mine and doeth them, shall be like unto a wise man who built his house on the rock; and the rains descended and the floods came and the winds blew and beat upon that house, and it fell not." The rains descended. The floods came. The winds blew, just the same as they blew on the Modernist world and on all those in the cults. But the difference is that Jesus is the Rock. He stands. Those who build their house upon the sand (sand is just a lot of tiny rocks, you know), the first thing you know they're shifting from one thing to another and always coming up with something different.

Many young people say they are colonies of love, colonies of freedom, freed from all the restraints of the past. In reality, they're free from nothing, bound tighter and tighter all the time. They're in the valley of death, in the shadow of death all the time, and they're trying to find some way to see some light at the end of the tunnel through which they are groping. Occasionally they catch an elusive, counterfeit glimmer, more frustrating than total darkness, because it never seems to get any nearer. This is because they have not found the true Light, the Light that shines in darkness, though the darkness refuses to recognize it. But the darkness can't overcome it. Just now, in the world, there's a tremendous covering of darkness over millions and millions of our population, and this darkness shall cover the earth, the Bible says. But there is also light, the light is coming on, and the light is getting brighter, and those people who have the light are walking in the light. They know they belong to another community. They do not belong to this world. They are foreigners, in this world but not of it. They're seeking another nation, another city, a city whose builder and maker is God. They are looking for the best and receiving the best. The Bible says, "the path of the just shall shine more and more unto a perfect day." So here we are in a world today where these two opposites occur all the time.

If we get into the dark, we are likely to get tangled up with any kind of strange doctrine, and somebody is always coming along with some new name. But Jesus is the Light of the world. He is the only Light of the world. Go to Him and He turns on the light in you.

I was in these dark fields. I know what these oppressions are. I know these feelings of bitter frustration. I know what it means to walk down the street and feel a great sense of doubt about anything until the point you feel, well, men aren't anything more than just a group of animals, highly developed animals, and when we are dead, we're dead, and that's all there is to it. Because evil takes out faith. Evil takes out trust. Evil takes out belief in Almighty God.

Then we come to Jesus, and He brings with Him, faith. He brings with Him, trust. He brings with Him, belief. As many as believe in Him, to them He gives the power to become children of God, born not of blood nor the will of the flesh, nor the will of man, but of God. You've got to be born again to bring on the light.

END OF THE SEARCH

5

End of the Search

After all the years of searching, after long years of exploring the fields of human knowledge and the occult, and after trying to experience things in the realm of the Psychic, I finally came to discover one day that I was not a Christian, after all. I would have considered it an affront if anybody had even suggested I wasn't a Christian. But I came to see that I was not.

Most of the people in the cults, Christian Science, Religious Science, Mental Science, are well-intentioned; some are even religious, but they are *not* Christians. At the heart of Christianity is the death of Jesus for our sins, and this they simply do not believe. To be a Christian, you have to accept Jesus, and what He did for you on the cross, and I had not done this. I went home feeling deeply disturbed, and I began to search where to find Him.

The story of Jesus meeting Mary and Martha at the time of the death of their brother Lazarus, is a revealing one. When Jesus came where Mary was, she said to Him, "Lord, if thou hadst been here my brother had not died." Jesus said, "Where have you laid him?" They said, "Lord, come and see." And then the great compassion and love of Jesus is revealed. He wept. So they came to the place where the tomb was, and Jesus said, "Roll away the stone." Martha said, "Lord, Lord. By this time his body decays. He's been in that tomb for four days. His body is stinking."

There is all too much 'stinking' thinking going on upon the part of Christians. We say, he's got a cancer; he's going to die. We say, that church is trying too big a thing; they'll never be able to pay for it. I can't get any place, because I have no faith. I can't be baptized with the Holy Spirit, because somehow I can't receive. All that is stinking thinking.

Jesus said to them what we must say to each other under this same thing. He said to Martha, "Said I not unto thee if thou shouldst believe, thou shouldst see the glory of God?" She became quiet. Jesus prayed and said, "Lazarus, come forth."

And, I think it must have taken a long time for Lazarus to get out of here, because he was all wrapped in graveclothes, all tight around. Here he came, stumbling out of the grave, and Jesus said, "Loose him and let him go." Those sisters must have been all thumbs as they unwrapped their brother and he was struggling out Finally he lifted up his arms, stretched them out. He was alive again. He had come from death to life. Now he could stretch out his arms better than he'd ever done in all his life before. He could feel the freedom of the atmosphere, the freedom of life around him, and the flowers and birds around him became more beautiful and more wonderful because now he was alive. He was alive to the glory of the Heavenly Father through His Son, Jesus.

I can imagine how Lazarus felt, because I, too, was in a tomb – the tomb of Modernism, Mentalism, Existentialism, which is just another form of Humanism. And I was in there with all the cultists, dead, nonproductive, making promises I could not and did not keep, no hope, no future, trying to lift myself up by my own bootstraps and doing absolutely nothing. I was dead in my sins; all wrapped up with the shroud of the cults, making empty affirmations and trying some way to demonstrate their truth. But nothing worked right. Nothing worked at all. I listened carefully. I read. I preached. I even taught it. And yet I received nothing out of it, and I never knew anybody who did. Once in a while somebody by some chance came across the path of one who had been successful in getting money or a partner, or in living a healthy life. But by and large, those people who had no health continued to have no health. And those who had no

- 58 -

wealth, continued to be poor. And those who had no partner, continued to live alone.

Oh, I continued to see this all the time, and I didn't get anyplace. And then one day Jesus said, "Ray Jarman, come forth," and I came out of that tomb. And Jesus said, "Loose him and let him go." And the one who was with me began to unwrap me, and he unwrapped and unwrapped and unwrapped, and finally my hands stretched out again. Oh, I was free. I lifted them up. I was free. I could breathe. I knew where reality was. I knew where the light was. The light was within me. I had come out of death, and I had stepped into life. Now I, for the first time, knew what life was.

But not all of the graveclothes were taken off of me at first. I remember going down to Long Beach, California, to speak to the Full Gospel Businessmen, and on my way back I said to Martin Hay, who was president of the club, "This thing you talk about — the second coming of Jesus, I can't receive. I can't accept that." You see, I had saturated my mind in the belief that this was just utterly impossible, and the years had proved that it wasn't true. He hadn't come in 2,000 years. What was the chance he was going to come in the next 1,000? No chance at all. I came to believe that whatever coming it was, it was a coming in spirit; that He'd come every time there was a crisis in your life, and you overcame that crisis, and that was the coming of Jesus into your life.

But the real, personal, coming of Jesus at the end of the age was completely discarded and was repugnant to my mind. Martin never said a word to me, for he explained later, ' I knew He who had started a good work in you, would perfect it unto the day of judgment." Not more than five weeks after that I was standing in the pulpit saying I could hardly wait for His Coming. More of the graveclothes came off.

Then I could speak the holy language of God. I knew the language of the Modernist. I knew the language of the cults. I could talk in their lingo, but I didn't know the language of God. And one afternoon at three o'clock, Ralph Wilkerson jerked off those graveclothes, and I began to speak in the supernatural language of God.

Now I know there are people who object to this. I know that they are strong. Some of them think it is a terrible thing, and I can understand this, because I once did. I thought it was the lowest kind of autohypnosis there is. I thought speaking in tongues was for the uneducated people of the world, that no intelligent people would do it, though I have seen university professors receive it since then.

But I spoke the supernatural language of God and it is a glorious experience. It's a wonderful thing. If we do the things He tells us to, He will do the thing He promised. If we do the things that are despised, God will set at naught the things that are. If we are willing to humble ourselves enough to speak in a language not our own, but the language of God, God will listen and hear what we are saying, and we will be filled with the Holy Spirit. This charismatic renewal is going all over the world today. While our newspapers are examining and wondering why people are leaving the churches, ministers are meeting in discussion groups to try to find the answer. They are saying that it is because the church is not relevant to life today, because the church is mired down centuries in the past, but none of them seems to notice that there's a group of people who are growing by the thousands, who are coming to the morning and evening services Sunday and several times during the week, and overflowing their churches, because they have found the power. The power of God in Jesus Christ, to be born again. The power to speak the supernatural language of God and to receive the indwelling of the Holy Spirit, is in them. This is the nature of the revival that is taking place, the biggest revival this world has ever seen.

The Bible says, the harvest is at the end of the age, and the greatest harvest of souls this world has ever known has already begun, because the age is coming to an end, and God keeps His Word. It used to be that if anything were happening religiously in the world, it was always in terms of the Catholic Church, the Protestants, or the Orthodox or the Nationalistic, but now something new is happening in the world — the great sweep of revival—and it is not in terms of any denomination or group, but in terms of all of them moving together. The Catholics, the Protestants together, receiving this tremendous new expression of God in terms of a personal experience.

When they receive this personal experience, they no longer ask, are you a Catholic, are you a Protestant, are you Pentecostal; they just simply talk as though they belong to the Lord Jesus Christ, and they are children; all of them, in the same family.

This is an entirely new expression. When you go to study this, you do not study in terms of psychology, psychiatry, psychotherapy, social psychology, or sociology. There is nothing. You study it in terms of an experience that is beyond any area of thought in our academic circles. Out in the general world, in the field of politics, the field of social action, it used to be that the church was a strong and integral part of everything that was going on. That's no longer true. The church no longer has a strong voice in anything, but the church now has a new relationship, a new culture that is apart from the world of things, apart from government, apart from sociology — in the world of a city that has foundations whose builder and maker is God.

Immediately the question is asked, "Aren't you interested in the social things that are going on, the social changes and the need for help to the underprivileged, the need for help to those who are maladjusted?"

Of course we are! But the answer to it is not going out in some kind of action, but in finding the Lord Jesus Christ who is the answer for everyone, and in this new-birth experience, whole new situations, new thoughts, and new sets of values take place, and the life becomes so changed that it moves into a society of the children of God.

If you go back to the history of the early church, you will find that it was a movement that moved around a personal experience. Something had happened to the people. And so it is now. A movement is moving around a personal experience. Something has happened to the people, and now they know Jesus Christ, not as an idea, not as a philosophy or ethics, but Jesus as a living, personal Savior who can save their lives through the shedding of His blood.

Strange as it may seem, vast numbers of churches of various denominations and students of religion seem to be unaware of what's going on in the American scene today. This tremendous movement of God – they close their eyes to it. They don't want to see it. They're trying to say it doesn't exist, but it does. And there's a tremendous return to the Gospel of Jesus Christ as it is given in the Word of God.

To practice the Word of God would seem utter foolishness, were it not so beautiful. It's not defensible in educational circles, nor in any field of knowledge. It's just what happens. It works. Wherever it is done, something happens to people. A piety and love for Jesus begins to burn so hotly within them that the coals begin to glow and even blaze.

Such a vast number have received this supernatural experience that the glow is being seen all over the world. There is a crass secular materialism in the Modernist church, but when we find this glow, the intensifying of the spiritual principle begins to make the church become spiritually alive, and the materialism begins to fade away. Before, it was the common aim to try to inherit the Kingdom of God and to build it up, to take it by storm, as it were; now, it's just receiving the Kingdom of God, because God has it to give even though we do not earn it. In the world, the world of things, the world of materialism, there's a filthiness and a vice that holy men do not permit themselves to think about. They have to move out of it. The baptism in the Holy Spirit does not take the person out of the world, but provides a new hope, new power, a new otherness that sends light over a dark world.

AFTERWARD

6

Afterward

One of the things that surprised and astonished me most was the way my congregation accepted my conversion. I had anticipated that when I went and told them what happened, they would be the happiest people in the world. They would say, "Look. Our pastor now has a *real* message for us. This is the thing we have been searching for."

But when I arrived there on Sunday morning, and I walked into that pulpit, I could see heads look back and forth at one another as if to say, something has happened to our pastor. They didn't know what, but they knew something was different about me. I could hardly wait to speak. The choir was singing and I could hardly wait for them to get through. And when they finished, I immediately stood up, and I told them that I had met the Lord Jesus Christ. I had actually seen Him. That He had actually put His hands on my shoulders and that I had been changed morally, spiritually and socially — in every possible way.

All my values had been changed. Things I once greatly despised, now I accepted in the Lord Jesus Christ. That the teaching I had been giving them for eighteen years was not the true teaching. That I would have to disown it and give them this new teaching. I begged of them to wait until they heard the whole story and could see what a change it would make in our congregation, our people and my ministry. But instead of that, many went out furious. They were disgruntled, unhappy and confused. Some turned back and said, "We've had enough of this. We don't want any more. I'm not coming back any more." I just accepted their fury and went on.

The Lord gave the Gospel to me, and I began to preach it every Sunday. I didn't even know I knew it, but it flowed out of my lips so freely that I made an altar call for commitment for the first time in my whole ministry. After fifty-two years of preaching, I made an altar call. And forty-eight people responded to the first altar call I made.

But as I went back of the door that day, one of my trustees said, "Dr. Jarman, you've spoiled and ruined the culture and refinement of this church. We're not going to stand for this!"

And they began to have secret meetings within a certain group in the church. They didn't tell anyone what they were going to do, but they were preparing the way so that they could ask me, who had founded the church, and brought in every development which existed in the church, to retire.

Well, the time came. On a Friday night, at eleven o'clock on August 17, 1966, they called me and told me that they had decided to retire me, and they didn't even want me back on Sunday. They knew that if I came back I'd tell the congregation what they'd done, and I would have. It would have been a mistake, but I'd have done it. I haven't been back since. I had a big church and I had a big salary. I don't have either one of them now. And, I've had many ministers come to me since that time saying, "Dr. Jarman, if I'd received what you've received, they'd kick me out of my church." And I've said to every one of them, "Who are you serving, your church or Jesus? I choose to serve Jesus."

It was generally circulated around that I had lost my mind. One colleague announced in his pulpit that I had become senile. Well, if this is senility, I wish to God I had become senile when I was twenty. But when this church was taken away from me, my salary and everything I'd depended on through the years, everything I had built, I said, "Lord, what do you mean by this? Why are you doing this to me? I have just found you and now you are letting me down. I haven't anything. I'm lost and sinking."

I didn't realize what was happening. The doors were just about to open, and as soon as I found the thing the Lord wanted me to do, doors have been opening ever since. I've traveled from one end of this country to the other, time and time again. I've spoken not in one, but in hundreds of churches, in many Full Gospel Businessmen's groups, in universities, in seminaries, in ministers' associations. I have seen ministers fall to the floor and beg God to forgive their souls. I saw one minister fall down on the floor and say, "Lord, I've made my wife into an atheist." And I thought, if he has done this to his wife, what has he done to his congregation? But he found the Lord Jesus Christ that day and is now going all over New England preaching the Gospel of Jesus Christ.

I had another minister cry out, "I hate the blood of Jesus." And before too long he was singing, "What can wash away my sins? Nothing but the blood of Jesus." This is a miracle, a miracle of God. One man at Louisville, Kentucky, said, "I'm a Presbyterian minister, have been one for thirty-five years. I've been preaching and teaching the very things you formerly taught, and I've known how empty my ministry was. I wasn't doing anything with anybody. I grew discouraged and disgusted, and I decided I'd have to give up my church. I asked God to take my life, and He wasn't willing to do it. So I guess I'm going to have to do it myself."

I said to this man, "Do you know the Lord Jesus Christ as you personal Savior?"

"I think I do."

"Oh, no, you don't. If you knew Him, you would *know* you do." I prayed for him then, and the Lord blessed him and saved his soul, and baptized him in the Holy Spirit. Now he, too, has returned to his pulpit and is preaching the Gospel and having the most successful ministry he's ever had in his whole life.

I've seen doctors and lawyers, undertakers, people of all professions and all religions — I've seen Catholic priests, Catholic sisters and members of the Catholic Church, receive the Lord Jesus Christ. I've seen Him transform and change their whole life. I have seen many people stand up and acclaim the name of the Lord. I've seen them hold up their hands and praise Him.

I had one man say to me, "Dr. Jarman, how can you stand these people holding up their hands and praising the Lord?"

I said to him, "Do you want to go to Heaven when you die?"

"Why yes, I do."

"You wouldn't like it, because that's what they're going to be doing, praising the Lord. They'll even fall on their faces and worship the Lord, saying blessing and glory and thanksgiving and honor and might, be unto Thee forever and ever, amen and amen. And, I want to get used to it. I want to be a part of that group. I want to proclaim His name, even if I have to fall down to the floor to do it, because this is a great blessing of God that God is blessing His people with these days."

A tremendous move of God, and what a change it makes! Confirmed Modernists, men of liberal education, men who have studied in the finest schools in America, are changing their lives.

I knew personally some of the outstanding professors of religion of the world. I studied under Henry Nelson Wyman of the University of Chicago, J. M. P. Smith, Edward Scribner Ames, Shaler Matthews, Shirley Jackson Case, and many other distinguished men of letters. I have heard their liberalism. I have seen their sociological historic approach to the Bible. I have seen how it has torn down the very foundation upon which the Bible has been made, and the emptiness and chaos and darkness that were left behind. I've seen it take away the power and the fire and the light and the glory of just knowing the Lord Jesus as our Savior. And then I've seen this come back, and I now say to you that the greatest proof of the reality of the Bible is not an intellectual one but a pragmatic one: it works when you receive it. And the greatest distress that comes to mankind, comes when it is taken away. That's the reality of the Word of God.

These liberals, who also call themselves Christians, have a right to preach whatever they want. They have a right to say that they are religious, because they are, and they are fine men, let me assert to you, some of the finest men I've ever known for their sincerity and their morals. I'll put them up against other professions, and they'll outrank them.

But goodness is not salvation. So I have found that as they receive the Lord and are changed, they are ready to discard all this higher criticism and lower criticism and historic approach to the Bible and begin to accept it for its Word, letter for letter, for what it says. A change and alteration comes into them, and into their church. If they are permitted to remain there, their church begins to prosper, and people begin to come in, to crowd in its doors, for this is the place where the action is today. This is the place where something is actually happening.

As a visiting speaker in a Pennsylvania university, I was participating in a panel discussion, when one young student spoke up and said, "Dr. Jarman, what about all these people of India; all these people who are followers of Mohammedanism, Hinduism? Are they all going to go to Hell? Are they lost?"

And I said to that young man, "I hear this question all the time. We always want to get away from ourselves. I don't know what God will do with these people. That's God's business. All I know is what the Bible says, and I consider the Bible the revealed Word of God. And the Bible tells me that I must come to God through Jesus. The Bible tells me I must recognize that I'm a sinner and that I must accept the blood of Jesus Christ to cleanse me from sin.

"What about you? Jesus one time said, 'If I had not come and spoken unto them, they had not have sinned, but now they have no excuse for their sins.' And so I say to you: if I had not come and spoken to you, maybe you'd have gotten through, but now you've heard; now you know the score. You wouldn't have gotten through to the rewards of Heaven, but perhaps there would not have been the strong punishment for your failure to accept Jesus, because you didn't know about Him. But now you know. It's not what is happening to the people of India. It's what is going to happen to you. We'll let God decide about the people of India, and the people of all the other religions of the world."

I have been a witness to literally thousands of miracles. I have seen legs straightened. I have seen withered limbs made whole and strong. I've seen eyes opened. I have seen cancers healed. I have seen other diseases said of doctors to be incurable, healed in an instant. God is moving. God is working today.

I never saw a miracle in the Mental Science groups. I've seen them put a towel over their arm and go around like a waiter at the table, with water in their hands, and I've seen them put oil on people's heads, but nothing ever happened. Nobody ever really got healed. Oh, some felt a little better, but no great healing. But, I have seen such healings that would astonish the eye; absolutely incredible. If I told you some of the things I've seen, you would doubt it yourself, and I wouldn't blame you. But I know because I've seen them happen. God is still in the healing business.

One of the most clarifying things that has come to me, has been the passage, "By Grace are ye saved through faith; that not of yourselves. It is a gift of God" (Eph. 2:8). By Grace are ye saved! Now, I used to believe that with some kind of study and accumulation of knowledge and service performed — a dedication of life to go out and clean up some community and perform a service such as washing somebody's feet, raking some old person's backyard or washing their clothes for them — was evidence of being a Christian. But it is so plainly said, "Not by works, lest any man should boast." It is not anything you could earn. If you could earn it, you could say, here it is, and you could take your ticket up to Heaven's gate and say, let me in, I belong in here. Here's my ticket. But *you* can't do it. By Grace are ye saved through faith — it's a gift of God. One you can't earn.

One you don't deserve, but one which through God's love you have received.

Then I have seen this marvelous power of Grace. Jesus was full of the Grace of God, the Bible tells us. "And we beheld His glory; Glory as of the Only Begotten of the Father, full of Grace and Truth. And John bore witness of Him and cried saying, 'This is He of whom I spake, for He that cometh after me is preferred before me; and His fulness have we all received, and Grace for Grace.' "

I think that word 'Grace' is one of the most marvelous words in all the Word of God. Cling to it. I know I'm not Holy. I never will be truly Holy. I want to be. I want to be a Saint of God, for that is what He has called us to become. I want to be the best one that God's got, but I'm far from it. I have this shining treasure in earthen vessels. I try to break the crockery apart to let the treasure pour out, for it is the Pearl of Great Price. It's full of Grace and Truth.

And Jesus was born full of Grace. He brought Grace to man. The law had failed, and all the things of the law had failed, and men discovered they couldn't keep the law. No one could keep the law. No one ever had. But Jesus brought a new one in, the Grace of God. And by this Grace we serve Him, and by this Grace we praise Him, and by this Grace our hearts are made full by Him. Everywhere Jesus moved in all of His career, He bestowed the Grace of God on people around Him. The Grace of God radiated from Him and flowed from Him into man. God was giving man something he did not in the least merit, but which would light his path for the rest of his life. Jesus was the Grace of God manifest (Luke 2:40). As a child, Jesus grew and waxed strong in spirit, filled with wisdom, and the Grace of God was upon Him. How marvelous it is to walk up to one that is full of the Grace of God, and more marvelous to have that one come up to you and put his hands upon you when he is full of the Grace of God. It brings in confidence, it brings in comfort, it brings in the knowledge of God, it brings to your remembrance all that He said, and it fills you with the Spirit

- 71 -

of God.

In the hours of pressure and frustration and destructions, obsessions of any kind, this Grace of God will come in and free you from the things of this world. You know, when Paul was preaching he went out from the Jews, and the religious proselytes followed him, and Paul and Barnabas, who were speaking to them, persuaded them to continue in the Grace of God. This is the thing we have to continue in. This is the thing so often missed. Some people hear the exactitude of hardhearted interpretation of the Bible, and they become frightened and turn away and say, "I can't do this, so I won't even try."

The Grace of God is the thing that makes it possible. The Grace of God forgives you, and the blood of Jesus is continually cleansing you; not once, but every day you are cleansed by the blood of Jesus Christ. This gives quality and reception to the teaching of the Word, that no amount of study, reading or instruction can do. See that you continue in the Grace of God; in season and out of season, continue in the Grace of God.

Wherever there is religious argument, vexation, debate, division within the church, it is literally impossible to hear Him, or see Him, and it is literally impossible to continue in the Grace of God.

Someone said to me, "Oh, that's too easy, altogether too easy."

Well, it is not easy to surrender. It is not easy to be a Christian. Wherever you find a group of people teaching that they are the only church and the only place where you can be saved, that all who do not believe the way they do are lost, these people know nothing about the Grace of God. Acts 15:10-11 says, "Now, therefore, why tempt ye God to put a yoke upon the neck of the disciples, which neither our fathers nor we are able to bear, but we believe that through the Grace of our Lord Jesus Christ we shall be saved, even as they."

The overflowing thanksgiving in my heart is for the Grace

of God, and that I can live on it both night and day, and I can carry it with me in that hour when all the soil of this world that has marked me in the past, shall be cleansed by the love and the Grace of God that saved me.

Formerly I was like a discarded dynamo, lying at the bottom of the ocean, just shifting around with the flowing of the tides, moved back and forth by the currents and the storms, but completely devoid of power and unable to generate any. But that day I was brought forth and connected up with the Grace of God, the dynamo was cleaned; the power began to move in; and it has been sending out its power ever since.

I had spent too long devoting my life to building a church, seeking a large membership, climbing the ladder of leadership and recognition within the denomination, though no amount of ascending could satisfy me. There was always something more to conquer, some higher place to reach, and I would come away disappointed. I moved in these avenues of endeavor, attained to a degree of success in them, but found they were only surface refuse on the disturbed waters of the denominations.

The horrifying sight, as I look back to behold it, was too great. The secularism of the church, the conflicts in it, the futility within it, the fruitlessness of it, how it all gave way to the finite and the ugly politics that there was at the core of the organization, and the pervading spiritual depletion. Nobody can get to speak in the coveted places, in the big conventions, unless they are politically accepted by those who were the ecclesiastical leaders. The outside edges of the place were full of gossip, political intrigue.

To look back on it now, I find myself absolutely repulsed by the whole idea. But then, to know the Grace of God is to see my weaknesses fall away. To see my heartbreak mended. To become a more effective pastor than I'd ever dreamed of being. To be able to pray full, rich, humble prayers. To see people healed under the hand of Almighty God. To be obedient to the guidance of the Holy Spirit. To see the Spirit of God move in people. To have brand-new goals and to start out on new crusades, the crusade to bring people to know the Lord Jesus Christ and the power of the Holy Spirit. These things brought blessings which seemed more than I could possibly contain.

Believe me, in all the years I've preached without believing in the Virgin Birth of Christ, and many parts of the Bible, thinking that the Bible was full of myth and legend and folklore, and the story of a tribal God, with many conflicts in it, I did not have a single convert. I had churches that numbered over a thousand in membership, but no converts. There was enormous activity, many organizations, counseling and psychologists and all kinds of efforts to fill lives with interest. There were bazaars, baking sales, rummage sales, suppers, men's clubs, women's teas and youth activities. But no one was introduced to the Grace of God. No one was trying continually to abide in that Grace. I was lying, unused, at the bottom of the sea of social action, ethics, and social intrigue, driven by the currents of social activism and denominational propaganda. I was the MC of a religious club.

But then one day when I was lifted up, I was drawn to the top, and I was cleansed — cleansed by the blood of Jesus Christ until I was gleaming and polished and regenerated, and I could see a new life and a new way, and a new goal, and a new meaning to my life, and the Lord gave the Holy Spirit to me, and that was the power, that was the beauty, that was the insurance. The thing that I had absolutely rebelled at, as I thought it was the worst kind of autohypnosis, for ignorant people. Now to see it move in my own life. I had once said that if I ever spoke in tongues I hoped I'd die. Well, I was dead already. I only came to life when it came to me. The shadows of doubt began sweeping away, and the light of truth began moving in my heart. I now had the Spirit, and the Spirit bore His witness in my spirit. All this came to me because of the Grace of God. It was the keeping care of God. I didn't merit it. I didn't earn it. I deserved the opposite. But God, through His mercy, love and Grace, gave all this to me. Praise His Holy Name for ever and ever.

A LIFE CHANGED

A Life Changed

I am often asked what in the world did you believe in and what did you preach? I had a basic belief that there was something divine in life itself. That some kind of an explanation had to be given of life, and to see life as it is on this planet you must know that there is something divine in it. I also believed that this divine life that was in man, was joined with the eternal life that is in God; that somewhere, somehow, there is something of God in everybody. Therefore, I believed that there was something essentially good in all human beings, no matter how bad they were, and if it were just possible to get hold of this essential good thing, we could transform any life.

I believed that man had evolved through the process of natural evolution, and I believed in the evolution of life itself. I believed that life itself had a growing evolution in it. I believed that man was growing in his ethical and social and governmental and moral life at all times, and while there were those on the lower fringes who were still carrying forth their animal heritage, there was a large group of people that was evolving into a higher behavior. I believed that as man grew in higher behavior, his own God-conception grew. That God, in other words, was a kind of following God. He followed our highest mind.

I believed also that God had revealed Himself in many ways and in many religions. That all of the religions of the world were some evidence of the revealing of this essentially divine thing that is in life, and that Christianity must not say that it is the only way, but one of many ways, and Christianity had no right to infringe upon those people who had some other religion; all religions should grow together in a kind of synthesis of religion.

I believed that there was a natural law in all life. That natural law was a law of love and the law of harmony. That good is better than bad. Kindness is better than cruelty. Love is better than hate. That these were natural laws, and to abide by these laws is to get the greatest good out of life itself. That as you abide by the laws and obey them, you go into the richness of life, and wherever you violate them, you pay the penalty because you lose the working of the universe.

I believed that Heaven and Hell were not places where you go after you die. Heaven and Hell were conditions in your attitude and the atmosphere of your life; the way you behaved. And this kind of atmosphere and behavior went on with you as you moved from this life to whatever there was in a life hereafter.

I believed that reason was the way to understand, that learning was the way, that the only way you can know truth is to learn more truth; that truth sets you free. And, therefore, as we search for greater knowledge we have a greater understanding of how to live. I believed that mankind would eventually evolve in that place where life would be much more pleasing to everybody and that it would be much more safe, and that it was the job of the minister to increase the rapidity of that growth so that the larger truth would come, and as you knew the truth, the truth would set you free.

I believed that religion could not change your nature, but could change character, and that, as we delved into religious thought, we were delving into that kind of thought that would provide the vitamins for character growth. And to grow in character is to grow in acceptance with man and God. I really believed that all things work together for good, but I did not include the line, "to them who are called according to His purpose." I believed in general good everywhere. Wherever it is, it works together to support, sustain, and produce for the advancement of mankind.

I believed in myself. I believed that because I am, I am

therefore the recipient of the greater laws of God, when I want to open myself to them. I believed in my own intelligence. I didn't consider myself the most highly trained person and the most intelligent person, but I believed that I had a natural gift of intelligence and that this natural gift was for the great masses of people. I believed that, in this intelligence that was naturally given to me and that I had earned through my studies, it was possible for me to impart what intellectual discoveries I had made; moreover, I had a responsibility to all mankind to do so.

I believed that because I am, God is. Anybody who exists has intelligence; he must have had some source of this comprehension, and that source was God. I believed in the goodness of God and the love of God. I believed that God could not create something greater than Himself, and since I am intelligent and have a natural desire for goodness, therefore, God must be better than I am.

But you see, all of this left out salvation. It left out Jesus as the Son of God. It left out that Jesus was born of the Virgin and therefore, as the Son of God, could die for my sins. There was no way of washing away sins, and the only way of freeing oneself from sin is through the process of growing intelligent and seeing how unwise it is to sin. Theologically, all Modernists, and I as well, are Unitarian in spirit, because we have denied the Deity of Jesus, and therefore, the whole Trinity loses its standing, and we believe only in God. We believe that God is love and that as we love we get closer to God, but we refuse to see that man is also a sinner, that his righteousness is as filthy rags, and that in him is a total depravity, and this total depravity can only be removed by man's being born again in Jesus Christ.

So when I experienced this great miracle, when the Lord Jesus Christ appeared to me, and He walked right up to me and I saw all the love in the universe in one single countenance, and I looked upon Him, He never said a word to me. He did not condemn me to Hell as he might well have done. He didn't move his lips. He merely put His hands on my shoulders and saturated me with the love I saw in His face, and something went out of me that did not come back, and something came into me that has never gone out.

From that day I was changed morally, spiritually, socially, theologically, and in my total beliefs. Everything was changed. I got down on my knees as a Modernist and came up a Bible-believing Christian, and that is a miracle. Now, I can see because my spiritual eyes have been opened. I can see how all these things that I so heartily gave my mind to and dedicated myself to, did not have the basic thing that all humanity needs: salvation through our Lord Jesus Christ.

I can see why people had grown tired and weary of the Modernist church. I used to stand up and say, "I do not believe in the Blood salvation." And, after all, that is the only kind of salvation there is, because without the shedding of blood, there is no salvation. I don't know *why* this is. I'm not sure any man does. There are things that God does not intend His children to understand, and the efficacy of the Blood is one of these Holy Mysteries. But I'll tell you this: I've seen *how* it works. When I see what the Blood salvation has done in me, when I see what happens in others who receive it, then I see that it is the only real thing in the world, the only thing that revitalizes life, the only thing that reestablishes morals, the only thing that corrects governmental disorganization and family troubles.

Now I no longer believe in the divinity of life. I believe in the divinity of God, and that when we are born again, He comes into us. He's not in us until we are born again, but when we are born again we become members of His family. We are born into His family. I no longer believe in the oneness with the Eternal, but I believe that man grows into a place when one day, one eternal day, we shall be like Him. We shall be one with the Father. And we are heirs of God and joint heirs with Jesus Christ. I believe the Bible means what it says; that we are heirs, not of what God has, but of God Himself, because as we grow in Him, we become like Him, in His image, and that is the eternal reward and the eternal blessing God will give us.

I know that man in himself is not essentially good. Man is essentially bad, and the lasting goodness that comes out of him, comes by the transformation of being born again in the miracle of Jesus Christ; we lift up Christ in our lives, and He draws the best to us.

I no longer believe in the process of evolution at all. I don't believe it is provable in any way, and I believe there is preponderant evidence that when God created man, He created with a decree of His own hand, and breathed into man the breath of life. At first I found it very difficult to accept the first eleven chapters of the Book of Genesis, until I came across the gap theory which plainly shows us that the world and great civilizations existed long before God created Adam and Eve, but because of sin they were blotted out and chaos and darkness and emptiness was on the world. God didn't create darkness or emptiness, nor chaos. God created light and order.

But when God came back upon this world, which had been destroyed because of the sin, then He reestablished a chance for man to come and live with Him. And He created Adam and Eve. Now I can understand all the eleven chapters of the Book of Genesis very clearly. They have opened themselves up and I can see, because when God said to Adam, replenish the earth, you can't replenish a thing unless it had been plenished before. So, therefore, I can understand this Word of God, and from this all the passages of the Old Testament and the New, began to clarify themselves.

I believe in Heaven and Hell. I believe in eternal reward in a Heavenly place. I don't know what it is going to be like. It is *not* going to be sitting on a cloud playing a harp, of that I am sure. There will be responsibilities, but there will be Heavenly order and there will be Heavenly harmony, and we will work together in a Heavenly harmony with God according to His plan and be totally pleasing to Him.

I believe that Hell is a punishment that will be sent upon those who, having been shown the light, choose to remain in darkness. I believe that to these there will not be any possibility of inheriting the good of God. Now, I do not believe that all will go into an eternal lake of fire to burn forever. That is for Satan and his angels and those who knowingly cooperate with them.

Modernists mean well. They are trying. Some of the finest and most dedicated men I know in the world are Modernists, but they are not going to receive the top rewards. There may well be differences in Heaven. We shall shine, the Bible says, as the stars in the Heavens, and some are brighter than others. I fear that the Modernists shall be relatively in the dark. Hell is lack of communion with God, and lack of association with God, and that will be Hell sufficient.

The primary purpose for living is not to search through reason for truth, but to become aware that Jesus Christ Himself *is* Truth, and if Christ shall set you free, you are instantly set free from all falsehood.

I still believe that denial of self through obedience to the guidance of the Holy Spirit is part of maturing in Jesus Christ, that there is more than just being born again and baptized in the Spirit. We don't stop there, but we go on and we *live* for Him. I'm looking for mature Christians, not manifest Sons of God. That's something for God to do. That's His choice. But, to grow in Him so we are pleasing to God, and one day when He chooses His own Manifest Sons of God, it may be that we will be among those chosen.

I still believe that all things work together for good to those who are called according to His purposes. I believe that whenever a person is born again, God has a purpose for him. He has a call for him. He has a witness for him to make. He has a plan for him to fulfill, and I believe that fulfillment is a part of our joy of living for Him. There is no time when one can believe in himself more than when he believes in Jesus Christ, because Christ comes to live in him. He's not in us until we join with Him. He says, "If you will abide in me, I will abide in you, and if you will abide in me, you will bear much fruit." And bearing much fruit makes one believe in himself. I no longer believe that intelligence, man's natural intelligence, is the avenue to God. I believe it's a miracle. It is being born again in Jesus Christ by a miracle, and that miracle gives to you the right to say to God, "I want wisdom."

"If any man lacketh wisdom, let him ask of God who giveth to all liberally, but let him ask in faith, nothing doubting, for he that doubteth is like the surge of the sea, driven by the wind and tossed." How can you ask in faith until you are in His family? And those who try mere intellectualism are driven by the wind and tossed.

I still believe kindness is better than cruelty. Love is better than hate. But I believe that kindness and love and grace, mercy, all come from God, and that as I receive Him, these elements of satisfaction and spiritual peace come from God and grow in me.

Now, the words that I have spoken in this book are not final. Nobody knows it better than I. I am just giving you a glimpse, a suggestion in the direction that will lead you so you can understand all these other errors. If you want to go into a greater study of them, you can do so. There are many fine books, quite well done, scholarly, and you can go to them and you can find the truth you are seeking. Two of the best that reveal the Satanic in various occult practices are the previously mentioned *Angels of Light* by Hobart Freeman (Logos, 1969) and *The Challenging Counterfeit* by Raphael Gasson (Logos, 1966).

I'm pointing out to you where I was, what I did, the search that I made, and how I came out, and what changes it made in me. And I'm telling you that only Jesus Christ could save me from that empty, living Hell.

Other books by Dr. Jarman: *Grace And The Glory Of God*, $1.50; *Supernatural Dreams And Visions*, $3.00.

Speaking engagements: *Write to*—CHRISTIAN CENTER CHURCH, Box 3000, Anaheim, California 92803

TA18 KATHRYN KUHLMAN — "AN HOUR WITH KATHRYN KUHLMAN"

TA19 KEVIN RANAGHAN, Author of **"CATHOLIC PENTECOSTALS"**

TA20 CHARLES SIMPSON — "A SOUTHERN BAPTIST LOOKS AT PENTECOST"

TA21 WILLARD CANTELON — "THE NEW WORLD MONEY SYSTEM"

TA22 THE CHARISMATIC RENEWAL —Bredesen, Ervin, Evans, Brown, Roberts

TA23 FR. JOSEPH ORSINI, Author of **"HEAR MY CONFESSION"**

TA24 PHIL SAINT, Author of **"AMAZING SAINTS"**

TA25 PAT ROBERTSON, Author of **"SHOUT IF FROM THE HOUSETOPS"**

TA26 MALCOLM SMITH, Author of **"TURN YOUR BACK ON THE PROBLEM"**

TA27 FRANK FOGLIO, Author of **"HEY, GOD!"**

RECORDS

MS120 AN HOUR WITH KATHRYN KUHLMAN $5.00

M7 NICKY CRUZ — 7″ record $1.00

M13-72 NICKY CRUZ — 12″ record $4.95

M125 NEW WORLD MONEY SYSTEM — Willard Cantelon $4.95

MS121 TAYLOR MADE CHARISMATIC MUSIC $4.95

order from your local bookstore
or W.B.S.,
Box 292
Watchung, N.J. 07061

SUGGESTED INEXPENSIVE PAPERBACK BOOKS
WHEREVER PAPERBACKS ARE SOLD
OR USE ORDER FORM.

A NEW SONG—Boone	AA3	$ .95
AGLOW WITH THE SPIRIT—Frost	L326	.95
AMAZING SAINTS—Saint	L409	2.50
AND FORBID NOT TO SPEAK—Ervin	L329	.95
AND SIGNS FOLLOWED—Price	P002	1.50
ANGLES OF LIGHT?—Freeman	A506	.95
ANSWERS TO PRAISE—Carothers	L670	1.95
ARMSTRONG ERROR—DeLoach	L317	.95
AS AT THE BEGINNING—Harper	L721	.95
BAPTISM IN THE SPIRIT—Schep	L343	1.50
BAPTISM IN THE SPIRIT—BIBLICAL —Cockburn	16F	.65
BAPTISM OF FIRE—Harper	8F	.60
BAPTIZED IN ONE SPIRIT—Baker	1F	.60
BEN ISRAEL—Katz	A309	.95
BLACK TRACKS—Miles	A298	.95
BORN TO BURN—Wallace	A508	.95
CHALLENGING COUNTERFEIT—Gasson	L102	.95
COMING ALIVE—Buckingham	A501	.95
CONFESSIONS OF A HERETIC—Hunt	L31X	2.50
COUNSELOR TO COUNSELOR—Campbell	L335	1.50
CRISIS AMERICA—Otis	AA1	.95
DAYSPRING—White	L334	1.95
DISCOVERY (Booklet)—Frost	F71	.50
ERA OF THE SPIRIT—Williams	L322	1.95
15 STEPS OUT—Mumford	L106	1.50
FROM THE BELLY OF THE WHALE—White	A318	.95
GATHERED FOR POWER—Pulkingham	AA4	2.50
GOD BREAKS IN—Congdon	L313	1.95

Title	Code	Price
GOD IS FOR THE EMOTIONALLY ILL —Guldseth	A507	.95
GOD'S GUERRILLAS—Wilson	A152	.95
GOD'S JUNKIE—Arguinzoni	A509	.95
GOD'S LIVING ROOM—Walker	A123	.95
GONE IS SHADOWS' CHILD—Foy	L337	.95
GRACE AND THE GLORY OF GOD —Benson/Jarman	L104	1.50
HEALING ADVENTURE—White	L345	1.95
HEALING LIGHT—Sanford	L726	.95
HEAR MY CONFESSION—Orsini	L341	1.00
HEY GOD!—Foglio	P007	1.95
HOLY SPIRIT AND YOU—Bennett	L324	2.50
JESUS AND ISRAEL—Benson	A514	.95
JESUS PEOPLE ARE COMING—King	L340	1.95
JESUS PEOPLE—Pederson	AA2	.95
LAYMAN'S GUIDE TO HOLY SPIRIT—Rea	L387	2.50
LET THIS CHURCH DIE—Weaver	A520	.95
LIFE IN THE HOLY SPIRIT—Harper	5F	.50
LONELY NOW—Cruz	A510	.95
LORD OF THE VALLEYS—Bulle	L018	2.50
LOST SHEPHERD—Sanford	L328	.95
MADE ALIVE—Price	P001	1.50
MANIFEST VICTORY—Moseley	L724	2.50
MIRACLES THROUGH PRAYER—Harrell	A518	.95
NICKY CRUZ GIVES THE FACTS ON DRUGS —Cruz	B70	.50
NINE O'CLOCK IN THE MORNING—Bennett	P555	2.50
NONE CAN GUESS—Harper	L722	1.95
OUT OF THIS WORLD—Fisher	A517	.95
OVERFLOWING LIFE—Frost	L327	1.75
PATHWAY TO POWER—Davidson	L00X	1.50
PENTECOSTALS—Nichol	LH711	2.50
PIONEERS OF REVIVAL—Clarke	L723	.95